The Boaz Method

How to Find Your Good Thing

The Boaz Method

How to Find Your Good Thing

John Alan Mack

Copyright © 2010 by John Alan Mack.

Library of Congress Control Number: 2010902879
ISBN: Hardcover   978-1-4500-5421-8
               Softcover   978-1-4500-5420-1

All rights reserved. No part of this book may be reproduced or transmitted in any form or by any means, electronic or mechanical, including photocopying, recording, or by any information storage and retrieval system, without permission in writing from the copyright owner.

This book was printed in the United States of America.

To order additional copies of this book, contact:
Xlibris Corporation
1-888-795-4274
www.Xlibris.com
Orders@Xlibris.com
59047

CONTENTS

I. INTRODUCTION 9
   History of My World pt. 7 10

II. WE DON'T NEED ANY HELP! OR DO WE? 13

III. STEP ONE—WATCH 15
    Watch Me *Watch* *19*

IV. STEP TWO—INVESTIGATE 21
    And What Were My Findings 22

V. STEP THREE—ENGAGE 23
   My "Engage" ment . . . Three Strikes, You're Out! 24

VI. A WORD ABOUT DATING 27
    A Date by Any Other Name 31
    Attractions 32
    Attracted? Not in the Beginning 35

VII. STEP FOUR—PROVIDE/PROTECT 36
     Blindsided 38

VIII. COURTING: THE RIGHT WAY, THE SAFE WAY ...40

IX. FOR THE DIEHARD ROMANTICS 43

X. WARNING! 45
   Now, about You 45
   I'm What! 48

XI. "A LITTLE HELP HERE . . ." 53

XII.	FINAL THOUGHTS	54
XIII.	ODDS AND ENDS	55
XIV.	INDEX	57

DEDICATION

I dedicate this book, first of all, to God, who made all of this possible by allowing His Son Jesus to pay the price for my sins and who made it possible for me to write this book.

To my wife Amia whose love and encouragement gives me the confidence to go forward with any idea I might have, no matter how difficult. With you by my side there is nothing I can't accomplish.

To my kids and their spouses, Joy and Brandis, Devin and Cashawn, Jonathan and Christina, and my fourteen year old Joshua; I hope Amia and I are living a proper example of what marriage should look like.

To the guys who have yet to take the plunge, I hope this book helps you understand the importance of marriage and gives you the tools you need to find your good thing.

INTRODUCTION

Don't be fooled! Don't get it twisted! Don't drink the kool-aid!

It's not the government, it's not Jerry Springer, it's not the palm reader downtown, it's not the guys you shoot basketball with every third Saturday, it's not your cousin Joe (I mean, dude, look at his life. Do you really want advice from Mr. Cheating-on-his-Fourth-Wife?), It's not even Oprah!

No one can give you the absolute best guidance, direction, counsel, or advice on finding the right person to marry than the one who created marriage in the first place.

GOD

This should be a no-brainer, but unfortunately it's not. OK, you tell me. If you want to know how the stealth bomber was designed to work, you wouldn't go to the guy that invented the Chia Pet, would you? No, you would go to the guys that designed the stealth bomber. You wouldn't go to the guy that came up with the pet rock to find out how the Jarvik artificial heart was designed to work, would you? Of course not, you would go talk to the inventor Dr. Jarvik himself. Or if you couldn't speak with him directly, the next best thing would be to read whatever he wrote on the subject.

Using the same logic, you would think that when we broach the subject of finding the right woman to marry, we would defer to the One who said, "It's not good that man should be alone," the One who said, "For this cause shall a man leave his father and mother and cleave unto his wife." Good grief; He's the one that *created* woman!

I think it's time we started seeking God's direction on the *front end* of all our decisions, rather than seeking His *help* on the *back end* after having made a bad decision. And if there is a decision more important than choosing a mate to live with for the rest of your life, other than accepting Jesus Christ as lord and savior of your life, I don't know what it is.

This book is the result of my desire to share with you how God led me through His word to find my "good thing," my helpmeet, the woman that would be my companion for the rest of my life, my wife Amia.

Now, is this another book on marriage? Absolutely, positively no, no, and, ah . . . , NO! This is the prerequisite course before taking Marriage 101. It breaks down this way; strong families begin with strong marriages which begin with a man making sound decisions based on God's word as to whom he chooses to marry. Starting this journey on the wrong road will waste too much time and gas, and time is not refundable and gas ain't cheap!

Although the concepts and specific steps I outline in this book come straight from God's word, please know that just like the concept of "You reap what you sow" is a biblical principle, it's a law that works universally. Most of the key principles in this book are biblical in origin, but they also have universal application. In other words, these principles work every time they're tried, no matter who's trying them. Having said that, let me quote a credit card ad that sums up my position on this, "Membership has its privileges."

This might be a good time to share with you part of my story of how the creator of the universe chose to step into the life of a regular Joe (actually my name is John) and guided my steps to find His choice of a helpmeet for me.

History of My World pt. 7

Without going into a long, detailed history of my life, suffice it to say, my life was pretty normal. Leaping to the relevant part, I got married at twenty-three. We had two fantastic kids early in the marriage and like too many people survived through a very "dysfunctional" married relationship for nearly twenty-four years. We had some highs, and lots of lows. Though there were a number of separations, divorce was never truly an option. Now don't get me wrong, we loved each other, but we were not a great match. We would have made great friends, but friends don't always have to agree on the *major* issues of life. Husbands and wives must. During the last three years of our marriage, my wife went through many major health battles, the last of which took her life. Even though our marriage wasn't what it could have been or even what it should have been, we did have some good times, and two great kids; and it is comforting to know that she no longer has to deal with her numerous health issues and is now in eternity with the Lord.

Then suddenly, after nearly twenty-four years of marriage, I found myself thrust into a strange new world. I'm forty-six with two adult children no longer living at home, and everybody's telling me, "You're still a young man (yeah, right) and you still have a lot of life to live." People even started talking about my not being too old to get married again, and I'm like, whoa, folks, pump your brakes. I didn't quite win an award for marriage the first time I tried it, so I wasn't looking to run back into that arena anytime soon. But all the while in the back of my mind I know that another word for widower is . . . *single* (cue the audience gasp and the soap-opera organ music).

So rather than deal with the *s* word (*s* word = single, come on, guys, stay with me), I came up with a one-year plan. I would take the next year to improve myself. After that, I would reevaluate my situation and see where I wanted to go from there. So I began to spend more time studying scripture, working on losing the flab (I have since picked some of it back up), and teaching myself how to play bass guitar. Fortunately, God had other plans.

Early into this time of self-improvement, the idea came to me, from God I realized later, to study the book of Ruth. The odd part was that I should study it from Boaz's point of view (I'll introduce him later). As I began the study, the hand of God began to move on my behalf. People began offering advice and information that proved critical to me finding my good thing.

Throughout the rest of the book, I will share more details about how the Lord walked me through the process of finding my good thing.

Well, enough introduction. Let's get to the info you're reading this book for. But *be warned*; this book will cause you to reevaluate yourself, challenge some of your long-held beliefs, and in the end cause you to slap yourself upside the head (yeah, I said upside) and say to yourself, "Self, this makes perfect, common sense. Why didn't I figure this out on my own?" To answer the question, first of all, common sense is no longer all that common. Second, there are so many roadblocks this culture, your friends, and even your parents may have put in your way; it's amazing anyone can *find* or *be* someone worthy of marrying.

OK, let's get to it!

WE DON'T NEED ANY HELP! OR DO WE?

You tell me. Just look around you. Look at the condition of the institution of marriage today. Marriage in America is no longer considered an institution, but marriages today *do* look like they've just escaped from an institution (get it, *mental* institu . . . never mind). Oh, so you think that was a little harsh, a little over-the-top? OK, so apparently you haven't seen the statistics on divorce. Well then, let's look at the numbers so we can all be on the same page.

It is generally accepted that the divorce rate in America is around 50 percent. This means, if you married that gorgeous girl you passed in the canned-fruit aisle at Walmart last week, chances are fifty-fifty the two of you will divorce. But you say, "She's so beautiful, her face is so pretty, her skin is flawless, and she smells soooo good, I would never leave a woman like that." This is precisely why I'm writing this book. Too many guys are using these same criteria in choosing a mate for life. For all you know, the fruit on the shelves may not have been the only "fruit" in the aisle at that moment.

What's worse is that the divorce rate for Christians is reportedly about the same as in the United States in general. How is this possible? How can those of us who claim to be followers of Christ and of the word of God fail so miserably in the area that is foundational to the structure of daily living that God has established? Well, in a word, selfishness. We have stopped striving to line ourselves up with God's will and have bowed to the god of popular culture. Why? Because we want what we want, period! Even though God's way is better for us (the manufacturer always knows how what he made will work best), we still want to do it our way. Well, I think by now we see what "our way" is getting us. We need to take a time-out, sit down with the playbook (the Bible), and get back to the original game plan. I promise you; you will end up in a better place than where following your own plan will get you.

As a former teaching minister at a church I attended, it never ceased to shock and amaze me how much the people of God either don't know, or how often they chose not to follow, what the Bible has to say about the major issues of life. We could have just finished a series on a particular subject and within days have people come up and ask in all seriousness, could we give them direction on how to handle the same situation we have just taught on? It's as if we as Christians are saying to pastors, preachers, and teachers, "I know what you taught on Sunday, but there must be another way to do this. I know you can't say it in front of the group [wink, wink], but you can tell me. What you taught us Sunday is not reasonable. What should I *really* do about this?"

The Boaz method is written to give you the tools you need to avoid the pitfalls and booby traps associated with finding *your* good thing.

Now before we move on, I need you to do something for me. I need you to go to the Bible and read the book of Ruth. Yeah, that's right, the whole book. It's a very small book, won't take anytime to read. Go ahead. Yeah, I'll wait . . . Finished? Good!

Now that you've done your homework, it's time to go to the first step of the Boaz method: *watch*.

STEP ONE—WATCH

(Without letting them know you're watching)

I can just hear it now . . . "Watch?!? Watch?!? What do you mean watch?!? Man, I've been watching women all my life. I've got it down to a science. I *watch* to find what looks good to me, then I *watch* long enough to figure out what's the best way to 'get in good' with her, then I become that guy. Next thing you know, I'm in. I got the woman I wanted." (Cue the big red *X* and the buzzer from Family Feud.)

For those of you who subscribe to the above technique, I have a question. How's that working for ya . . . honestly? Sure, you can find a woman using that technique. You may even luck up and find an OK woman, but I thought the idea was to find God's best, not just anybody that has two *X* chromosomes. (Is it two *X* chromosomes, or two *Y*s, or an *X* and a *Y*, or . . .) You don't really have to do anything to find just any woman, but I thought you wanted to raise the bar, go for the gusto, shoot for the moon, leave it all on the field—sorry, got a little carried away. Where was I? Oh yeah, *watch*.

Now the first step in the Boaz method is watch (without letting them know you're watching). Here's a news flash. Write this down. Every woman is not wife material. Some aren't now, but will grow into it later. Some will never become wife material. Shocked? You shouldn't be. Deep down you already know this, man. You're just too afraid to admit it to yourself, or anyone else for that matter. Here's the problem. If you *are* watching, you are probably watching the wrong thing. Watching a woman's pretty face, beautiful hair, or nice shape does not constitute proper watching. Now let me be perfectly clear. Chapter 2, verse 5 shows that Boaz noticed Ruth first, and he obviously liked what he saw because he went on to find out more about her. So yes, a woman's appearance is important, and yes, we men are visual, but that's not enough to start laying down your rap, mack, game, *(insert current term here),* and establish a romantic relationship with a woman you know little to nothing about.

What you *are* looking for are character traits. This is an important concept; a person's true character shows when he or she thinks no one is looking and especially when they think no one they want to impress is looking. They may be more open around their friends, but a potential suitor? Absolutely not! This is why you must do the bulk of your watching in stealth mode. I'm not saying you have to stand in a corner of the church, store, library, etc., with a pair of binoculars, watching a woman's every move (binoculars . . . hmm). I'm also not talking about following her home to see how often she takes out the trash and what's in it. This is "stealth" mode, not "stalker" mode. So now the question becomes, "What should you watch for?" Good question! To answer that question, we need to go to the operator's manual (the Bible. C'mon now, stay with me) and see what characteristics Boaz was able to identify in Ruth that made her a draft-lottery pick.

1. *She chose God.* Chapter 1, verse 16 says Ruth turned her back on the god of her people, the Moabites, and chose the god of the Israelites. The Bible says the following,

> Be ye not unequally yoked together with unbelievers (2 Corinthians 6:14)

    That's about as plain and clear as you can get. If you don't get this one right, it's pretty much downhill from there. If you want God in it, she must have God in her. It absolutely amazes me how often guys who say they are Christians marry women who are either not Christians or do not exhibit Christian morals or a Christian lifestyle. Then after a short time, with a shocked expression on their face say, "I never thought she would do something like that!" or "I don't know why we're constantly fighting." or "Why did I get married in the first place?"

So exactly what part of "Be ye not" do we not quite understand? Is it the *be*? The be is speaking of a state of being, something that you are. Now if you tie *not* to the be, you get "Do not be something" or "Don't be something."

Maybe it's *yoked*. This term literally refers to an apparatus that "binds" two animals at the neck, which is then attached to a plow. This allows the animals to pull the plow to till a field. This setup works fine if you have yoked or "bound" two of the same type of animals together. The problem arises when you yoke two different types of animals together and then attempt to till your field. If you yoke an ox with let's say, a donkey (careful), you have unequally yoked two animals together. These animals are not only different in size, but also in strength, speed, temperament, and even stride length. By the time you've finished plowing your field with this ox and donkey (careful), *if* you ever finish, you probably would have completely missed planting season. In the context of this verse, and for our discussion here, *yoked* refers to not being married (the apostle Paul uses the term *bound*) to someone who is not a Christian. How often have you seen marriages that didn't work out because one of them was a believer and one was not? They have two different value systems, two different worldviews. They are "bound" to fail.

Maybe it's the Old English. Maybe the part we don't get is the *ye*. Sometimes people get thrown by *thee*, *thou*, *ye*, etc. This one's easy. *Ye* means "you"! Put it all together, you get "Don't *you* marry a woman who is not a Christian." Questions? Good. Moving on.

2. *Loyal*. Rather than go back to her home country to fulfill her personal desires and find a husband, she stays with her mother-in-law (chapter 1, verse 16). That says a lot about how important family is to her. It also speaks of how committed she will be to you.

3. *Hard worker*. In chapter 2, verse 2, Ruth shows a willingness to work. She didn't ask Naomi to go with her, she wasn't waiting for a man to show up and take care of her, and—this next point is huge, so write it down—she didn't use sex as a tool to get her needs met. In this culture, sex sells everything, or should I say, sex is the "drawing

card" or the "worm on the hook" that is used to lure you in and get you to hang around long enough to become interested in buying the whole package.

Be careful; don't take advantage of her willingness to work (no pimps here). Rather, look at it as a sign that she will be an able partner in scaling whatever mountains and responsibilities your future family may face.

4. *Respectful of men*. Chapter 2, verses 10, 13—in these verses you see Ruth showing respect to Boaz, in verse 10 bowing before him, and also calling him *lord* in verse 13.

Fellas, you don't want to find out one, three, seven years into your marriage that the reason your family is not progressing the way it should is that your wife has little to no respect for male leadership in the home, or anywhere else for that matter. Unfortunately, because of what women have been taught over the last thirty-plus years, this particular characteristic will be much more difficult to find. Not impossible, but difficult. This is one of the areas where you need to have God on your side. He can help you to avoid making some disastrous choices. Remember, although God is helping, it's still your job to do the legwork. He won't do it *for* you, but He will do it *with* you.

Here's a list of just some of the things you should be watching for: how she carries herself, how she handles her children (if she has any), how she handles her personal affairs. How does she handle the things of God, the people of God? How does she communicate her love for God (if she has any)? Are her conversations with or about men laced with respect or disrespect? Are her conversations full of vulgarities? See, we've gotten this thing backward. We don't start finding out about the real woman until after we've gotten emotionally (and too often physically) attached to her. Next thing you know, you're getting married, then having kids (or vice versa), and you find yourself attached for life to a woman that has no real relationship with God, no respect for you, and more issues than a ten-year subscription to *People* magazine.

Watch Me *Watch*

After the Lord sent me to the book of Ruth to find the principles I'm sharing with you in this book, I began to apply the first step, *watch*. Now there were a couple of things I did prior to beginning my watch. First, I compiled "the List" (I'll cover this list later). I also decided that I would begin my search at the church I was attending, so I got another list. This second list contained the names of all the single women who attended the church, and no, it wasn't called the hit list (but that is pretty clever). Once I got the list, the first thing I did was to shorten the list by eliminating women that I already knew enough about to believe they would not work out. Does that sound cruel or harsh? You're not picking someone to play hopscotch with. This is not a game. As former British prime minister Margaret Thatcher is reported to have said to President George H. W. Bush around the time of the First Gulf War, "Don't go all wobbly on me." What better way not to hurt some young lady's feelings than to make a pursue-or-not-pursue decision prior to getting emotionally involved with her. Now where was I . . . oh yeah.

So I began watching some of the single young (not too young) ladies at church. After a period of time, one woman began to stand out from the crowd. We'll call her "Lisa". Lisa was a regular. She was involved with a couple of ministries at church and from a distance seemed to be someone that was serious about her walk with Christ. I decided to move on to the next step (coming up). As I began to find out more about her and have *friendly* conversations with her, something strange happened. Lisa disappeared. Someone who was a wouldn't-miss regular at church Sunday morning and Wednesday night suddenly disappeared. I didn't see Lisa again for a number of weeks. Eventually, during this period of not knowing what happened to Lisa, I decided to begin looking around to see if there was anyone else who might fit the bill.

The following Wednesday night, I noticed a young woman up front speaking to the group that night. It then popped in my head, "Hmmm, what about her?" I had noticed her around church, but I thought that she was married. After finding out she wasn't married, I started the same friendly getting-to-know-you, nice-guy approach toward her. Now before you ask, I'll tell you. Yes, I noticed she was attractive; actually I'd say she was cute but not before I noticed other more important things about her. Appearance was not on the top of my list; it was on my list, but not even in the top three. This is also a very important point; hold on to your desires regarding her appearance with a very loose grip. You may find that the woman that is the best helpmeet for you may not have every physical attribute you desire. Having said that, I will say that I have found God to be very gracious and will honor you with some of the desires of your heart, when you put His will for your life first. I can honestly say that I put my trust in the process that had been laid out before me through my study of the book of Ruth. Since I was not in any hurry, I was willing to take my time and let the process work itself out.

This brings up another very important point. Don't rush the "finding" process! I know we live in an "I wanted it yesterday" world. ASAP is no longer any good; now it must done BHP (before humanly possible). Save the microwave for popcorn and leftover two-day-old pepperoni pizza, and let the work of finding your mate-for-life take the amount of time needed to do it right. In my case, the right amount of time totaled about one year from first phone call to honeymoon. Your results may vary, but I'd say three months is too soon, and three years is too long. You may know she's the one after three weeks, or you still may not be sure after eighteen months. Just remember it's hard to get a full picture in less than three months, and if you still aren't sure after year two or three, then you're probably not applying yourself, and you've lost interest or slipped into neutral.

STEP TWO—INVESTIGATE

Time to put on your Sherlock Holmes hat, monocle, and pipe, and get to work. (Just don't go out in public looking like that, OK?) You need information, and you need it NOW! Oh, and don't wear the Columbo-looking trench coat; you don't want to look like a flasher.

In Proverbs 22:1, the Bible says,

> A *good* name *is* rather to be chosen than great riches, *and* loving favour rather than silver and gold.

The next step is to investigate. When Boaz decided he liked what he saw (physically, and anything else he was able to learn by "watching"), he took the next step. He investigated Ruth. In other words, he found out what type of reputation Ruth had. In chapter 2, verses 10 and 11, when Ruth asked Boaz why he was being so nice to her, he repeated what he had been told by other people. He said she deserved to be treated well because of how she treated her mother-in-law Naomi and because she had left her people and her god and joined with Naomi's people and Naomi's God.

Now to some people this may seem like gossiping, but the word *gossip* is defined as "the spreading of rumors, trivial or sensational (usually malicious) information." You don't want rumors or sensational information to be repeated to others, but an idea of what type of name she has made for herself in the public. Think of it as filling in the blanks in an application for employment because she *will* fill the position of the person that will most help or hinder you in fulfilling God's will for your life. She will also affect positively or negatively your family's reputation and name. Proverbs 31:23 says,

> Her husband is known in the gates, when he sitteth among the elders of the land.

This entire chapter of proverbs is advise that King Lemuel got from his mother that he is now passing on to his son. From verse 10 to the end of the chapter, King Lemuel is telling his son what type of woman to look for. The verse above comes from that chapter. This verse is describing the type of woman that is such a benefit to her husband and home that she makes it possible for her husband to be known by the leaders (movers, shakers, and decision makers) of the city. In others words, she created an environment for her husband to be successful. This may be where we get the old saying, "Behind every great man is a great woman." Unfortunately, the converse can also be true, that a man's wife can be a prime contributing factor to his failure.

Remember, Proverbs 22:1 says, "A good name is rather to be chosen than great riches, and loving favour rather than silver and gold." How will the wife you find affect yours?

And What Were My Findings

What's interesting about this part of my story is how much information was volunteered about Amia without asking. I think that this too was God's hand of influence in my life. Looking back it appears that 99 percent of the information I was given about Amia was right on the money, and all of it was positive. I was told she was a good woman, serious about her relationship with Christ, a hard worker, and a good mother. I also found she was intelligent, articulate, and highly respected by the members of the church and at her job. She passed this checkpoint with flying colors.

STEP THREE—ENGAGE

Engage, not *engaged*! Good grief, man, calm down (think about switching to decaf). An important part about investigating is getting information directly from the person herself. The Bible says,

> A good man out of the good treasure of his heart bringeth forth that which is good; and an evil man out of the evil treasure of his heart bringeth forth that which is evil: *for of the abundance of the heart his mouth speaketh.* (Luke 6:45, KJV; italics *mine*)

In other words, if allowed enough time to talk freely, most of us will share/expose most of our deeply held beliefs, opinions, and secrets—good or bad. But you, Sherlock, must be willing to listen, really listen. Given enough time, you will learn more about her than she would otherwise ever be consciously willing to share.

Now you're not getting this information to use against her, or to spread around to everybody you know. (You are a man of integrity, aren't you?) You're trying to find "the one," the "right one," and you need all the help you can get. Remember, this is for keeps. The word of God says,

> But don't begin until you count the cost. For who would begin construction of a building without first calculating the cost to see if there is

> enough money to finish it? Otherwise, you might complete only the foundation before running out of money, and then everyone would laugh at you. They would say, "There's the person who started that building and couldn't afford to finish it!" (Luke 14:28-30, NLT)

The point is, if you start something big without putting in the proper planning and preparation on the front end, it is a guaranteed disaster, and people *will* laugh at you. And we're not talking about just any old building; we're talking about the most important "structure" in human civilization, the family. And the foundation—the first part of the structure that is done, that determines how well the rest of the structure will hold up under duress—is the marriage.

If the marriage/foundation is messed up, being laughed at will be the least of your worries. Too many men and women have lived, and/or are now living, pain-filled lives simply because they took the subject of marriage and finding the right mate lightly. And it is not only they who will suffer, but their children also suffer. Then, because children live out what was modeled before them by their parents, they go out and create the same marriage relationship they grew up seeing. And the cycle begins again.

Now before we all get so depressed we go sign up to be monks, let me clarify something. Some of you (and you know who you are) may be wondering whether or not engaging a woman in information-obtaining conversation is done before or during the dating relationship. You may even say, "Isn't that what dating is all about?" The next section is for you, a section on the proper dating techniques to use while following the Boaz method, a section I like to call "A Word about Dating." But first let's check on our hero and find out how he fared in engaging Amia.

My "Engage" ment . . . Three Strikes, You're Out!

Once I decided to go further with approaching Amia, I began to engage, or attempt to engage, Amia in conversation. My friendly nice-guy approach was failing miserably. For the next couple of weeks after church, I would try to engage Amia in a conversation, only to find myself talking to someone who was only lightly involved in the conversation and would never stop moving toward her car. This clearly wasn't doing anything for my self-esteem. I finally decided to give it one more shot, and when I prayed about it, I said, "OK, Lord, if it doesn't work this time, then she must not be the one and I'm moving on." I also decided to change my approach. Rather than trying to build up to it, I decided to just come right out with "I would like to get to know you better, can I get your phone number and call you sometime?"

The following Wednesday night after Bible study, I caught up with her and said, "Look, I've been trying to connect with you using the nice-guy approach and it's not working, so I decided be blunt and just come right out and ask you, I would like to get to know you better, can I have your phone number?" Little did I know she had been on to my interest in her for some time. In fact, she knew I was up to something the very first Wednesday night I began to consider her. Not only that, but she had asked the associate pastor to walk her to her car so "Brother Mack won't try to talk to me." She even went so far as to have an "I'm not interested in having a relationship with you" speech ready to go the next time I tried to talk to her.

So what happened? She gave me every phone number she had including her mother's. (I'm a baaaad boy . . . no, not really.) Why? Was it because I was so smooth? Was it because I'm so good-looking? (Well, I am good-looking . . . no, not really). God intervened. This is where faith comes in. If you're being lead by God and *His* word to do a particular thing, follow His instructions. Then you must trust that He will make it work out for you, and intervene if need be.

I put my trust in the process because the process came from God. I knew it would work better than anything I could come up with on my own.

And now, as promised, a word about dating.

A WORD ABOUT DATING

DON'T!

(That is *a* word isn't it?)

OK, OK . . . stop yelling . . . give me a chance to explain. (Sheesh!) Now I know that the don't-date thing really threw you off, right? Right. So tell you what. Let's bounce this dating idea around a bit and see if we can come up with something that makes any sense.

First of all, let's look at most people's idea of dating.

Your name is Joe. You're just a regular guy who is not ready to get married. You're just interested in dating (fooling) around, having some fun, seeing what's out there. Somewhere in the future, if you happen to fall in love with someone, cool, but you'll cross that bridge when you get to it. You don't plan on having a serious relationship anytime soon. You're usually seeing two or three girls at the same time, but hey, you're not looking to get serious, so it's OK. A few years pass, and you're still just dating around. There were a few girls that you kinda really liked, but they didn't work out for whatever reason. There were also a few girls that really liked you. A couple of them got really emotionally attached. You, on the other hand, got *lucky* and slept with a lot of them. You may get married one day, but hey, why buy the cow . . . ?

Now, let's look at the typical Christian approach to dating.

Your name is Jeff. You're a Christian guy who is not ready to get married just yet. You're just interested in dating around, having some fun, seeing what's out there. Somewhere in the future, if you happen to fall in love with someone, cool, but you'll cross that bridge when you get to it. You understand the importance of marriage, so when you're ready for marriage you'll get a bit more serious about what you're doing, but of course, you're not there yet. You usually only date one or two girls at a time, but hey, you're not looking to get serious, so it's OK. A few years pass, and you think you might be ready to get serious. There were a few girls that you kinda really liked, but they didn't work out for whatever reason. There were also a few girls that really liked you. A couple of them got really emotionally attached. You kinda, accidentally, ended up sleeping with a couple (actually a few) of them. You know you shouldn't have, but hey, nobody's perfect and you had good intentions so . . .

Trust me; this is not fiction. I've personally known or are aware of way too many guys like these two examples (and you know a bunch too).

Unfortunately, even for Christian men this is the rule rather than the exception. The current idea of dating as many girls as possible until you're ready to settle down is an extremely new concept historically and definitely the least effective way of finding a mate for life. Actually, dating in our current culture primarily works to allow a person to have meaningless sex with as many people as possible with as little emotional investment as possible. I compare the effectiveness of contemporary dating to the following example:

Let's say Bruce is interested in eventually buying a new car. He decides to test-drive a bunch of cars until he's ready to buy, but he really has no idea what type of car he wants. He's not even sure if it's a *car* that he wants. So he spends the next number of years test-driving cars, trucks, SUVs, motorcycles, mopeds, in-line skates, Heelys, etc.

After a number of years, Bruce figures out what type of car he really wants. He thinks he has come to an intelligent decision regarding what type of car he wants based on all the "great experience" he gained from years of test-driving anything and everything he could get his hands on. What Bruce doesn't pay any attention to is the damage he left in his wake. "What damage?" you ask. (You ask really good questions.) Well, Bruce is a selfish driver, so in the process of test-driving all these different "modes of transportation," he . . . scratched some, dented some, totaled two, stripped the gears in the first motorcycle (he never rode one before), ran out of gas in the moped and left it on the side of the road, and lost a wheel to one of the Heelys.

The other problem Bruce doesn't realize he has with all the "great experience" he supposedly gained is, what yardstick or baseline was he using to help him separate the good from the bad modes of transportation? Was he relying on something his dad taught him, or some unsolicited advice from some of his buddies (most of whom have done their own share of damage to modes of transportation), or did he just come up with something on the fly off the top of his one-order-of-fries-short-of-a-Happy-Meal head?

One reason why Bruce is described as a selfish driver is because he doesn't really know the true value of the *right* car. If he knew the true value of the right car, he probably wouldn't have scratched some, dented some, totaled two, stripped the gears in the first motorcycle (he never rode one before), run out of gas in the moped just to leave it on the side of the road, and lost a wheel to one of the Heelys. He's having too much fun enjoying himself.

The other reason Bruce is selfish is he believes if the car he picks doesn't work out for him, he can always trade it in for another one.

But when a man understands how valuable the right car can be, he will do his research in advance because he knows doing his research on the front end will save him time, trouble, and heartache (and money) on the back end. He won't waste time on a car that does not meet his criteria. He won't be talked into a car that does not meet his criteria. Once he finds the car he's been searching for, he will only take the time necessary to verify that what he has found truly does meet his qualifications, and then he will move quickly to finalize the deal.

Wait a minute. Did you read that right? Did you see the word *criteria* in the previous paragraph? Am I talking about a list of predetermined qualifications that a woman must pass before she would be considered for the position of helpmeet? Absolutely!

Now I know that the idea of having a list of qualifications sounds kind of harsh and emotionless, but just like in our car analogy, it only makes common sense to have a plan for any major decision we would make. But again, common sense is not that common.

A Date by Any Other Name

Did Amia and I date? Yes and no. Did we go out on what one might call dates? Occasionally yes. Did we date? Using the typical definition, no, we courted. In other words, within the context of a relationship based on an established goal of marriage (courtship), we went on dates. A date is when two people who have a greater interest in each other than friendship, go somewhere to enjoy each other's company. The prime difference between courtship and dating is courtship has a predetermined and communicated goal which is marriage. Dating has no predetermined goal. Dating has a "let's see what happens" type of construct. Amia and I courted, and within that courtship, we went on dates.

Hope that clears things up a bit (or muddied it up dramatically).

While we're on the subject of dating, I want to address something that I think most guys take for granted and don't even consider as an area of concern. This is the issue of attractions.

Attractions

What is it that first attracts you to a woman? ("She's breathing" doesn't count.) What is it about a woman that if you see her across a room, or pass her in a hallway, or meet her in a group of friends, causes you take notice and think you would like to get to know her better. Is it her eyes, is it her smile, her hair, is it how she fits into her so-tight-they-must-have-been-spray-painted-on-in-a-stiff-breeze jeans?

I can relate. I was a face man. A cute face was my thing, especially if she had dimples or almond-shaped eyes. I was also attracted to—and don't laugh—an overbite (I asked you not to laugh). Not so big an overbite that if she ate an ear of corn, she would eat the back row first, but a slight overbite was very cute to me.

Don't misunderstand my point. As I said earlier, a woman's physical appearance has its place, but did you happen to notice that anything on your list that can be observed across a room, or in passing, or within five seconds of meeting, has absolutely no bearing whatsoever on the quality and character of the woman you have just decided you'd like to get to know better? And let's not fool ourselves; on the last couple of pages we've described what most guys mean when they say "get to know you better."

Here's the problem with attractions being the basis of you deciding to initiate a serious relationship with a woman.

First, an attraction-based relationship creates too great an opportunity to become emotionally attached to someone who may not be God's choice of a mate for you. I know you're thinking, "It's not like that out here these days. We don't become quickly or easily attached to one another like that. Even if there is a short-term physical relationship (sin), or friends with benefits (sin), or even if it's a longer relationship that is physical (sin) or not, we just don't get emotionally attached very easily these days." BALONEY! Write this down; burn it into your memory. You can *and will* become emotionally attached to *anyone* if given enough time and opportunity.

Now read that last sentence again.

Now read that same sentence again.

Get it? Got it? Good.

For example, how many times have you seen, in a guy/girl friendship, over time either the guy or the girl or both develop feelings for the other person? They may be seeing other people at the time, but it never fails to happen. This is the main problem with the dating culture and why the divorce rate is so high. Dating creates an environment that is highly conducive to creating emotion-only connections. When a marriage is based on an emotion-only connection as opposed to a commitment-based marriage, you can hear the ticktock of the clock counting down until the marriage self-destructs. Remember, half of all marriages fail under our current dating culture, even Christian marriages.

My second example of attractions, and why you must not base a serious relationship on them, is kind of personal to me and maybe to you too.

Have you ever been attracted to a woman, and you can't put your finger on exactly why? She doesn't have the type of looks that you are normally attracted to. You don't have anything obvious in common. No common interests, no common background, nothing. Despite all the differences though, you follow your normal pattern to make a connection with her. After a period of time, you find yourself in situations or environments that, except for your involvement with her, you would never place yourself in. If you're lucky and haven't gotten deeply emotionally attached, you find yourself looking for excuses not to see her. Eventually, if you're lucky, the "relationship" ends, and you move on. Unfortunately, what happens usually is one or both parties do get emotionally attached. How many guys have married girls they really would not have married if not for the emotional attachment that developed from some unnamed attraction that then led to the emotional attachment? The world may never know because the guys won't tell, but again the divorce rate is an indication.

For me, my attraction problem was plain old garden-variety lust. There was a period during my college years, prior to salvation, when I was trying to hit any woman that moved (sorry, slang term. Hit: "have sex with"), but not consciously. I wasn't aware at the time that that's what I was doing. The strange thing is that at the time, I didn't have a clue as to why I was attracted to girls I had little to nothing in common with. I just knew there was an attraction. At the time, I honestly thought my motives were pure, and though I couldn't explain the attraction, I expected to develop a real relationship. It wasn't until after I had slept with them that I suddenly realized I had no more interest in having that type of relationship with them (I see you nodding your head with that "How did you know?" look on your face). It wasn't until recently that I have come to understand what that was all about. There was nothing good, right, or proper about it. It was all lust based.

What guys never talk about is the damage we cause young women (and ourselves) who then carry that hurt and mistrust into other relationships and even into marriages. I pray that God moves in their lives and heals them of the pain and the memories that our selfishness caused.

To those that I have hurt, I apologize. I am truly sorry.

For you it may not be a sexual attraction. For you it may be an attraction to girls that are needy. Someone you feel sorry for and want to rescue. That's a noble sentiment, but not something to build a strong marriage on. You may be attracted to "mother" types, someone who will take care of you and pamper and spoil you just like an overprotective mother does. For others, you may be attracted to introverted women with low self-esteem. Someone you can dominate and rule with an iron fist. Understand that properly executing the role of a godly husband would create spiritual and natural growth in his wife, not fear and isolation. Whatever the attraction is, if it causes you to make decisions and compromises that you know are not good or right, be polite, apologize for wasting her time, and break into a Joseph-running-from-Potiphar's-wife sprint for the nearest exit. Then spend some time seeking to understand and correct the issues you may have that causes you to have these types of attractions. Trust me, you'll thank me later.

Attracted? Not in the Beginning

When I think about it, I wasn't physically attracted to Amia. Actually, my thoughts toward her never even entered that area in the beginning. I guess I was so committed to not using physical attributes as a determining factor in considering someone that I didn't really process the fact that Amia was and is very attractive. It wasn't until I finally got that phone number and actually started talking to her that I realized how attractive she was and how attracted I was to her. This, of course, opened up a whole new can of worms.

I think we've talked enough about what's wrong with the typical dating scene. So what does a guy do if he's not going to date? (Another great question you've posed . . . I'm really impressed.) I don't want to get too far ahead of myself, so we'll save that for later.

STEP FOUR—PROVIDE/PROTECT

I know you're going to think I'm crazy (if you don't already think that) as I describe the next step(s) in the Boaz method. As you notice I combined two steps, provide and protect, in this section. I combined them because they are basically interchangeable. It doesn't matter which one you do first. You may even find that they may happen simultaneously. Provide and protect cover two of the most basic needs every woman has: the need to feel loved and the need to feel secure. Something that we all must understand, guys as well as women, is that *love*, correctly applied, is actually a verb and not a noun. Love is not some tingly feeling in your stomach (that *could* be last nights' sausage pizza with extra anchovies). Love is an action based on a decision and a commitment to live out that decision. This book is an attempt to try to correct many of the mistakes we have made choosing mates based on emotions, ignorance, and indigestion, all of which will pass (pun intended) over time. The most well-known verse in the Bible is a perfect example of true love. John 3:16 (KJV) says,

> For God so **loved** the world, that he **gave** his only begotten Son, that whosoever believeth in him should not perish, but have everlasting life. (emphasis mine)

God "loved" and then "gave." God's love for the world was expressed by action, Him giving His only Son so we won't have to perish (protection) and that we can have everlasting life (provision). This is the same pattern Boaz followed in his early dealings with Ruth. Nearly half of chapter 2 describes how Boaz provided food for Ruth and also how he protected her by not allowing the young male workers to bother her in any way.

Now I know that when you got to this chapter, your first thought was probably "Provide? Protect? I'm not married to this woman! I'm not even engaged to this woman! Why would I want to provide for or protect someone I'm not married to?" (Another great question.) Well, let's look at the information Boaz was working with when he decided to provide for and protect Ruth.

1. Boaz finds an attractive young woman gleaning in his fields.
2. She shows humility in how she asks for permission to glean in his fields.
3. She shows a willingness to work and do what is necessary to help her family (even her mother-in-law).
4. She shows respect for Boaz by bowing before him and asking why she has found such favor in his sight.
5. She had an excellent reputation in the community.
6. She converted to the God of the Israelites.

In other words he had in his midst a good woman, a godly woman, a virtuous woman. So what's a single God-fearing man to do when he finds a woman who is USDA Prime wife material? If you want to be lumped in with all the other knuckleheads out there, then invite her to a John Mayer or Maxwell concert (dating mode, not good). Or you can do what Boaz did and present your case as a man worthy of greater consideration (courting mode, very good). Boaz began to provide for and protect Ruth. He began to prove, by his actions, that he could meet two of Ruth's most basic needs and in doing so identifies himself as USDA Prime husband material.

So then the question becomes, "How do you provide for and protect a woman you are not married to and just getting to know?" Well, at this point we should have already decided whether or not she has cleared the first "checkpoints" (nicest way I could put it), and if she has, these are the next steps to take. You've been watching this woman for a period of time, and if you've been paying attention, you've noticed areas of her life where she could use a little help. It could be something as little as you noticed that she is a really hard worker who doesn't take much time for herself, so you could spring for tickets to the latest chick flick for her and (no, not you) a couple of her girlfriends to go see. She may be driving on her spare tire (doughnut), and you decide to take her regular tire to get it fixed, then switch out the tires yourself while she watches. (You can change a tire, can't you? Can't you?) You may find that she's going through a tough period financially (a lot of that going around) and choose to help her out by paying a bill, filling the gas tank, or buying some groceries to put in the fridge. If you're paying attention, and your heart is right, ideas will come to you. Just make sure you make the offer in a nonthreatening, no-strings-attached kind of way.

Some guys will say the goal is to get the woman to take care of you, not the other way around. Remember, this is for MEN, REAL MEN! NO PIMPS OR PLAYERS ALLOWED! This is for men who know the real value of a woman as God created women to be, and men who understand that a true woman should be provided for and protected and that the right woman will help him to be all that he was created to be. Also, don't be afraid of being taken advantage of. Just because you are in provide-and-protect mode doesn't mean you've stopped watching her. You never stop watching. Before "I do," you're watching for who she is. After "I do," you're watching for ways to please her, meet her needs, and prove to her that in your life she is second to no one but God. If she is the type of person that takes advantage of people, you want to know this earlier rather than later.

This is your opportunity to be that guy you dreamed of being when you were a little kid—the superhero, the knight in shining armor. You remember, don't you, daydreaming about beating up all the bad guys and rescuing the lovely damsel-in-distress?

Blindsided

It was a Friday night. I was on my lunch break. It was my first time to call Amia. I thought she would be at home, but she was still at work. Before I finished that phone call, my hearts' desire was to protect Amia from the stressful world of work that she found herself locked into. I could almost say a protective attachment developed after the *first* phone call. I didn't expect this, wasn't prepared for this level of emotional involvement anywhere near this early into the relationship. Remember, I had already done investigative work on Amia, so at this point, becoming attached wasn't a problem. Also, I was committed to the process God had laid out before me, so my antennae were still up looking for red flags. My problem would have been missing a good woman while looking for a robot that fit perfectly into my prerequisites, not getting too attached to one woman. Someone may say, "That sounds so cold and calculating." My only answer to that is *it worked*.

Amia was a very self-reliant woman, so offering to pay for certain things were not received as well as expected. Where I was able to provide for Amia was her older Honda Accord. Oil changes, spark plugs, and other vehicle services were where I was able to be the hero and come to her rescue. In general, just looking out for her best interest is how I showed my desire to protect her, including sharing large amounts of relevant but worthless information of which I had tons (she was impressed by it then, she's just amused and slightly annoyed by it now).

COURTING: THE RIGHT WAY, THE SAFE WAY

What follows might be somewhat controversial (as if some of the previous stuff wasn't). When we think of courting versus dating, we usually think of courting as something that happens after you have dated someone for a while and decided that you have found the woman you want to pursue to possibly marry. Actually, I define courting as establishing an exclusive relationship between a man and a woman, with the *predetermined* goal of identifying whether or not the two of you are compatible for marriage. What I'm saying is I believe courting is the only honest, safe, and considerate process by which a couple can most effectively move toward marriage, and eliminate dating altogether. You're probably thinking that courting is an old-fashioned, antiquated, and just plain dumb concept that has no place in this modern world. I'm not talking about your parents arranging your marriage for you, even though that still actually happens in the United States (and getting your parents' sage advice throughout the process is a very good idea), but what has this modern world's process gotten us? High STD rates, high abortion rates, terminal bachelorhood, and a 50 percent divorce rate. This modern world may have produced some great tech-toys, but it has also produced some terrible marriages. You tell me what's better, a great HD signal of the biggest game of the year on a fifty-two-inch flat-screen plasma TV, or spending your entire adulthood with the love of your life? 'Nuff said.

I'm not going to give you a detailed layout on what to do in a courtship, but I will give you some parameters and guidelines to follow.

Begin with the end in mind. You must remember you are entering into courtship with one goal in mind—marriage. If you keep this in the back of your mind as you walk through this time, everything that you do, plan, or think will fall into its proper place. This will help you maintain the proper level of respect, not just for the young lady you are walking through courtship with, but also for the institution of marriage, and even for yourself. It's amazing how good you feel about yourself when you are doing the right thing the right way.

You must have an exit strategy. This part of the process, no one wants to think about, but it is actually key to the whole concept. While going through the courtship period with a young lady, it is entirely possible one or both of you will decide to end the courtship. Since this is preferable to the alternative which is to date, get emotionally attached to, and marry someone you hardly know, both of you should come together in the beginning of the courtship period and decide what can be deal breakers and how the problem will be addressed. Deal breakers should be limited to character traits or behaviors that speak to character traits, foundational belief systems, or life goals that are incompatible with no hope of reconciling the differences.

Safety first. You want to do the right thing in every step of this courtship, right? Of course! So then you won't mind putting in some safeguards and rules to keep everything good and godly, right? (What was that? Excuse me . . . I'm sorry, I can't understand a word you're saying through all the mumbling, stuttering, and stammering you're doing.) Sex before marriage is a sin, period. Even if you're courting, even if you're engaged. To keep from putting yourselves in a situation where temptation can take control, the two of you must take control on the front end and establish some ground rules. You want to keep from being alone for extended periods of time, especially at night. You do not want to have discussions about sex at any time, in any way. Not face-to-face, by phone, via e-mail, smoke signals, nothing. Be aware that certain types of movies can generate romantic feelings that can lead to other things. And under no circumstances can you, at any time during the courtship or prior to marriage, listen to any songs by Luther Vandross.

Give as good as you (want to) get. Do you want her to fully commit to the courtship process? Fully commit to it yourself. Do you want full disclosure from her? Be totally open yourself. You must be everything in the courtship you want her to be. Both of you must commit to putting your all into it; otherwise, you might as well be out there taking your chances with all the 50%'ers. If at any time you feel she is not giving 100 percent to the courtship, address it immediately and expect her to do the same. Moving forward with those types of questions in the back of your mind will damage anything good you're trying to establish.

Honesty is the best policy. This should be self-explanatory. This is one of the main reasons you're not doing the dating thing. The dating scene feeds off lies and deception. Putting your best foot forward and masking all your imperfections (lies and deception) are prerequisites to "successful" dating. We are trying to avoid being a 50%'er, we're not trying to guarantee being one.

Build on a solid foundation. God must be first in both of your lives. The first thing on my "wife wish list" was that she loved God more than she loved me. This should be at the top of her list as well as yours. The reason is this: if I'm at the top of her list, everything she does will be based on her understanding of what I need and what I want, which may not always be what's best for me, her, or the family. If, on the other hand, her desire is to please God first, then everything she does on my behalf is going to reflect God's will for me, us, and the family, which is perfect. Also, remember the foundation is the first thing that is done before a home is built. There is some "groundwork" you must do before you begin to build your home. We'll go into more detail on this point later.

FOR THE DIEHARD ROMANTICS

Now, some of you still think the way a guy is supposed to find his wife is to meet someone (however that happens), date, fall in love, and then marry her. We've all heard of people "falling in love"; it may have even happened to you before, but, fellas, I'm going to need you to help me out on this one. I need you to follow my thinking on this.

OK, correct me if I'm wrong, but isn't falling something that's *always* been considered a *bad* thing to do? Stay with me here. *Falling* into a puddle of mud, bad; *falling* off a bicycle, bad (I've got the scars to prove it); an airplane *falling* out of the sky, very bad. Even something as "romantic" as a shooting or *falling* star is just a piece of space rock entering into our atmosphere and burning up (that doesn't sound like a good thing either).

I remember as a kid growing up in South Bend, Indiana (Go Irish! . . . sorry), we would go on vacations to visit out-of-town relatives almost ever year. One summer I remember hurriedly going back and forth between the house and the car remembering things I forgot to pack. On one sprint back to the house, I tripped over the front porch step and *fell* into and through our new aluminum screen door. The pain and embarrassment from that fall is all I remember about that whole vacation. Don't remember where we went, who we saw, or what we did, just the hole in the door, the cuts, and the laughs. So now you're telling me that the same word that brings about memories of pain and embarrassment in every other instance is supposed to engender thoughts of love, joy, and lifelong companionship when you *fall* in love? I don't think so.

Looking at the condition of marriages and the divorce rate today, I'd say it's still bad to fall!

Summoned to Court

Amia and I talked on the phone for two weeks before seeing each other outside of Sunday and Wednesday at church. Before those two weeks were up, we knew we loved each other. We began discussing a wedding date after about a month. This is not typical. Your results may vary. We originally set the date for one year later in May. We later changed the date to ten months later because we knew we wouldn't last that long. Yes, we were very physically attracted to each other, so we had to maintain boundaries and limits to keep from crossing God's lines. She only came to my house twice. Both times I had to pick up something, and so we weren't there for more than an hour either time. Amia fell asleep in the living room both times (my presence was so overwhelming . . . no, not really). We went out to dinner a few times, but mostly we spent time together at the house Amia shared with her mother and sister. The greatest, safest environment known to man is the home of your fiancée's mother.

WARNING! PLEASE READ THE FOLLOWING INFORMATION *BEFORE* PUTTING THE BOAZ METHOD IN GEAR

I know this is near the end of the book, but this section is the most important section in the whole book. Your success in using the Boaz method will be directly related to how well you apply the information you are about read. Some would even say this should have been the first section of the book.

Now, about You . . .

Throughout this whole book, we've been talking about what you should do to find the wife of your dreams and God's guidance in that process. What we haven't talked about is who this guy is that's doing the finding.

Remember when we talked about finding a woman that is USDA Prime wife material? Well, the question becomes, "Why would a good and loving God, who when asked for bread would not give a stone, who when asked for a fish would not give a snake (*Matthew 7:9, 10*)? Why would this good and loving God give a woman who is USDA Prime to a guy who is mystery meat!" Any USDA Prime woman who is seeking to be married is not asking God for mystery meat. She is praying for USDA Prime husband material. Your first mission, if you choose to accept it, is to develop yourself into USDA Prime husband material. Before you give first thought to finding a wife, you must first become a man worth marrying. You won't arrive at perfection, but perfection should still be your goal.

Let's go back and take another look at Boaz because the description of him given in scripture says a lot about what he was and what you need to be.

The first verse of chapter 2 introduces Boaz this way,

> And Naomi had a kinsman of her husband's, a mighty man of wealth, of the family of Elimelech; and his name was Boaz.

The first thing we see is Boaz was related to Naomi's husband. Naomi's husband was a Jew, which makes Boaz a Jew. Who were the Jews? They were God's chosen people. If God created marriage, and He did, and Boaz was one of God's people, and he was, and you want to follow Boaz's pattern for finding the right wife, and you do, then doesn't it make sense to be in the same relational position with God that Boaz was? So the question becomes, how's your relationship with God? Would God give the same response to this question that you give? There is so much more to a relationship with God than just finding a wife, *so* much more, but for the sake of our discussion I'll confine myself to the subject at hand (we can talk about not going to hell and the other things later).

Again, membership does have its privileges. God intervened in Adam's life when he said, "It is not good that man should be alone," then he gave him Eve and thus established the institution of marriage. God intervened in Jacob's life when his father Abraham had his eldest servant go out to find a wife for Jacob and the servant prayed that the woman that should be Jacob's wife would come out to a well and offer him *and* his camels water. This is how God brought Rebekah to Jacob. God intervened in my life when on my last-chance effort to establish a more-than-acquaintances relationship with Amia, when I asked Amia for her phone number so we could get to know each other better by talking (novel idea—talking on the phone to get to know one another, not dating which encourages designed deception), little did I know she had already planned to tell me she was not interested. Next thing she knew she's giving me every number she has including her mom's number. To this day, she still is amazed by what happened. God chose to involve Himself in the life of a barely average Joe, to help me find the right woman for me.

Second, Boaz is described as a "mighty man of wealth." Now, I'm not going to say that before you find a wife you must amass a Bill Gates- or Donald Trump-sized fortune, but I will ask you this question. Are you currently gainfully employed? Do you have a job? Do you have your own place to live? I know that due to the current condition of the American economy, getting a yes to these questions is not as easy as it once was, but choosing to marry before establishing your own living arrangements and finances is like driving a car before getting your driver's license and car insurance. You may be able to enjoy the benefits right now, but you're setting yourself up for some real problems down the road. So are you going to have a home and financial structure already established before finding your wife, or were you planning on moving her in with you and Mom until the *both* of you get the money and housing thing figured out? Now, you're not one of "those" guys are you? You know 'em. The ones that think it's cool to lay up in the woman's home, eat up the woman's food, and spend up the woman's money, and bring nothing to the table but some torn-up underwear. The Bible calls these types of women "silly women" and this type of guy a whole list of bad things. It would be a good idea to see what scripture actually says about this type of situation,

> This know also, that in the last days perilous times shall come. For men shall be lovers of their own selves, covetous, boasters, proud, blasphemers, disobedient to parents, unthankful, unholy, Without natural affection, trucebreakers, false accusers, incontinent, fierce, despisers of those that are good, Traitors, heady, highminded, lovers of pleasures more than lovers of God; Having a form of godliness, but denying the power thereof: from such turn away. *For of this sort are they which creep into houses, and lead*

captive silly women laden with sins, led away with divers lusts, (2 Timothy 3:1-6, KJV; italics mine)

Not very pretty. These are not words that I would want used when describing me, and I know this doesn't describe you (or does it?), so let's move on.

Don't think that the idea of a guy having a house and a job first before getting married is something I came up with. Actually, I stole the idea from God (I didn't really steal it, I just . . . you know what I mean). It comes from the order God placed things in Adam's life. All this comes from Genesis chapter 2. First, in verse 8 God gives Adam a place to live, the garden. Next, in verse 15, God gave Adam a job to do, to take care of the garden, " . . . to dress it and keep it." In verses 21-24, God gives Adam a wife. Notice the order of events here. God gives Adam a place to stay and a job before He gives him a wife. I think this is significant. Don't read the wrong thing into this order of events. The order does not identify priority; it identifies chronology. It identifies what should be established in a man's life before he gets married. Many men prioritize their job above the marriage, but you can't square that with scripture. The Bible clearly teaches the preeminence of marriage above all else in the family structure. Yes, even above the children (don't ask. We'll cover that in my book on the family). Too often we think we have all this great wisdom and we can come up with our own stuff, but if we would take time to seek wisdom from God's word, we would know that many of our ideas are just plain dumb. We would avoid many pitfalls if we were more willing to get counsel from God before we jump in the pool. Then we could find out the pool was drained for repairs the easy way, rather than finding out from experience the hard way. And by the way, experience is not the best teacher; it's the hardest teacher.

I'm What!

As you build the most important part of the foundation for your future family, *you*, there's some information that you probably haven't been given that you need to know to do this thing the right way, God's way. You might want to sit down. From God's perspective, when it comes to what happens within the family unit, God considers the husband to be the responsible party. In other words, He holds the man responsible for whatever goes down in the family (don't *look* at me in that *tone* of voice). Right now, everything you have been taught by this culture, your friends, maybe even your parents, is telling you that this is wrong. You're thinking, "We are no longer in the Dark Ages, we're enlightened. Men aren't supposed to rule over women. Everything is equal now, fifty-fifty. The husband and the wife are to share the responsibility in the family. That's the way it's supposed to be." OK, first of all I didn't say men are to rule over women. Second, when did mankind's enlightenment become equal to the Word of God? If we are going to take a position on a subject, if we are going to choose sides, shouldn't we take God's position on . . . well . . . *everything*?

So where did I come up with such a crazy idea? Well, to find it, we need to go back to where this concept first started. To do this we need to go back to the year . . . one, or thereabouts.

It's the beginning of everything. Adam has been created, and he's been doing his job of taking care of the garden. He recently finished naming the animals and found there was no animal appropriate for him, and he was alone, so God made Eve just for him. Eve has just had her fateful encounter with Satan, who has talked her into considering eating from the tree of the knowledge of good and evil. We'll pick up the scripture narrative from here.

> And when the woman saw that the tree *was* good for food, and that it *was* pleasant to the eyes, and a tree to be desired to make *one* wise, she took of the fruit thereof, and did eat, and gave also unto her husband with her; and he did eat. And the eyes of them both were opened, and they knew that they *were* naked; and they sewed fig leaves together, and made themselves aprons. And they heard the voice of the LORD God walking in the garden in the cool of the day: and Adam and

> his wife hid themselves from the presence of the LORD God amongst the trees of the garden. And the LORD God called unto Adam, and said unto him, Where *art* thou? (Genesis 3:6-9, KJV)

Now follow me because these next points are keys to understanding the position of responsible party. Question: who did the serpent (Satan) trick into eating from the tree of the knowledge of good and evil, Adam or Eve? Correct. Eve was tricked. Question: who was the first one to actually eat the fruit, Adam or Eve? Correct again. Eve ate first. Question: who convinced whom to eat the fruit, did Eve convince Adam, or did Adam convince Eve? Correct again. Eve talked Adam into eating the fruit. Final question: whose name did God call when he made the scene? Adam! This is not insignificant; Eve allowed herself to be conned by Satan into doing something she knew God said not to do. Eve was the first one to eat the fruit from the tree of the knowledge of good and evil. Eve was the one who talked Adam into going against God's will and eat the fruit, but when God shows up and calls a name (of course He already knew what happened) the name He calls is Adam's. Now to us, the fair thing for God to do would be to deal with Eve first, since she did the most damage. Maybe He would even deal with Satan first because he started the whole thing. Instead, He calls the name of the guy that wasn't involved until the end of the whole deal, Adam. Why? Because he's the RP.

Let's use an analogy from the corporate world. Say you have a department in ZYX Company not performing up to established standards. The VP over that particular area decides he needs to address the situation in order to improve performance. Will the VP talk to the individual employees first, or will he first talk to the department manager? He will first talk to the person that is responsible for that area. He will first talk to the responsible party. Why did God call the name of the person that was least involved in "Fruit-Gate"? Adam was the RP.

The second point, to me, is even bigger than the first, but you have to look a little closer to catch it. Near the end of verse 6 you see where Eve ate first then Adam ate. Verse 7 begins with "and the eyes of them both were opened." So their eyes were not opened until Adam ate.

This is huge! Is it possible that if Adam had considered the amount of responsibility he carried and not eaten the fruit, we could right now be living in the garden, enjoying God, life, and family without issues and problems? I believe so. In case you were wondering, everyone in this situation received consequences for their actions, but the husband was the one called on the carpet for what happened. God asked three questions, where are you, who told you you're naked, and have you eaten from the tree. He only asked questions of Adam because Adam was the RP.

Right now, you may be rethinking the whole idea of getting married. You may be thinking that if you have to go through all this, then it's just not worth it. I say you couldn't be farther from the truth. Not only is this not a lot to go through, but the rewards of a godly approach to finding a wife are so huge that you will realize how little effort it really takes to reap such great benefits. You may think, how can I say it takes "little effort" when I had to write a whole book on the subject? But when you think about it, the only thing you have to do is change the way you think about marriage, dating, and courtship. (Oh, is that all?) Once you've started that process, everything else makes sense and follows along easily. The Bible says,

> And be not conformed to this world: but be ye transformed by the renewing of your *mind*, that ye may prove what *is* that good, and acceptable, and perfect, will of God. (Romans 12:2, KJV)

And

> For as he *thinketh* in his heart, so *is* he: (Proverbs 23:7, KJV; italics mine)

In other words, don't settle for the way the world does things and follow along like mind-numbed robots, but change to a new way of thinking that lines up with the will of God. When you change your mind, your heart will follow; when the heart changes, the corresponding actions happen automatically.

Also, understand that in the process of preparing yourself for marriage, I'm not saying that you have to fully complete the Mr. Perfect program before you actually start looking for your good thing. I am saying that these things must be moving down the tracks when you begin looking. Am I saying you must have the career job, working for the company you will retire from before you begin? No, what I am saying is you must be gainfully employed before you identify a "person of interest." Am I saying that you must be planning to build an addition to the four-bedroom, two-and-a-half bath colonial with a pool that you own before beginning? No, I am saying that before you attempt to lead in a home with a wife and possibly kids, you learn how to lead yourself and be a good steward of your own money, in your own place for preferably six months to a year, before you bring in a wife who has her own ways of thinking, living, and handling money.

There is less work in planning to avoid problems before you start than fixing problems after you have started.

"A LITTLE HELP HERE..."

Before I finish, I need to reiterate a point that I've made more than once in this book. We can all use a little help in areas of our life, and this is one area where we need all the help we can get. In chapter 2 verse 3, the Bible says that when Ruth went to find a field to glean from, her "hap" was to end up in Boaz's field. So Ruth just *happened* to end up in Boaz's fields, with Boaz who just *happened* to be a kinsman-redeemer to her, who just *happened* to be a wealthy landowner, who just *happened* to be interested enough in Ruth to provide for her and protect her, who just *happened* to be willing to challenge another kinsman-redeemer for the opportunity to marry Ruth, who just *happened* to be in the lineage of Jesus Christ. There are way too many just-happeneds in this for me to believe it's all just a bunch of coincidences. In fact, I believe the reason the story of Ruth is even in the Bible is because it shows God's desire to bless the lives of those who choose Him. Ruth could have decided to follow Naomi's advice and go back to Moab with her sister-in-law Orpah and try to find a husband there. If God had not involved Himself in my search, I am convinced I would not have found Amia.

Say it with me . . . (wait for it) membership . . . has . . . its . . . privileges.

FINAL THOUGHTS

Statistics prove that many of the ills of society stem, at least in part if not totally, from the disintegration/dysfunction of the family unit. Teenage pregnancy, crime, and drug use are all societal problems that primarily come from an absent or disconnected father, or the inability of both parents to work together to properly raise their children. Marriage itself is under attack from multiple sources. Culture says it's better to live together than get married. The tax code says it's cheaper to live together than marry. Even the definition of what marriage is, is under attack.

A strong family begins with a man and a woman properly coming into agreement and then becoming one. The problem comes in when the proper groundwork has not been done to assure the best possible marriage relationship. It has been said thousands of times, but it is still true and poorly adhered to: if you fail to plan, you plan to fail. It's true in business, and it's true in marriage.

Two guys, you and someone you don't know, enter the county building, smiling and holding your fiancées' hands, seeking to purchase a marriage license. One of the two of you guys entering the building will divorce the woman whose hand he is holding.

Which one will you be, the one who will remain married for life or the 50%'er?

Don't be the 50%'er

Don't be "that" guy.

ODDS AND ENDS

Boaz by the Numbers (after having read the book)

1. Pray. Not only do you want to pray about your future wife, you also want to ask God to show you the areas in your own life that hinder you from becoming a godly husband.
2. Begin the process of becoming USDA Prime husband material.
3. Read all of Proverbs 31. This will give you an idea of important characteristics to look for in a wife. Also read all of Proverbs 6. This will give you an idea of some things to avoid when looking for a wife.
4. Make your list. This is the "what I want my wife to be/have/look like, etc." list. Prioritize the list with number one being most important on down to least important. You will of course include things like Christian, not currently married, not currently on death row. Also include personal preferences like eye color, body type, interested in sports, etc. You will be amazed how God will give you some of the desires of your heart when you make what's important to Him your top priority. Below you will find examples from the list I made before I began my search.
5. Start the process. Enjoy the ride. Prepare to be amazed by what God will do on your behalf.

The List

What follows are some of the items that were on my list. I can't include everything because some of them were very personal. Another reason why I can't include them all is because I can't remember them all. Some of the items on my list were daydream-type stuff that I really didn't expect to get because they weren't on God's list. This brings up an important point. You must be willing to give up your personal preferences. In fact, your personal preferences should not be a factor in whom you choose to consider. What God did for me honored my desire to be pleasing to him, by giving me all but one or two of all my personal preferences down to the tooth. Literally! Remember my thing about teeth? Amia has the cutest little gap between her two front teeth. I love it! Anyway, here's part of my list:

1. Must love God more than she loves me.
2. If she's divorced, it must be a biblical divorce.
3. Must have a biblical understanding of the roles of husband and wife.
4. If she has any kids, they must be adult children. (This is one I didn't get, and I'm happy about that. Joshua is about to turn fourteen and is a great kid, and I love him a lot.)
5. Something about body type (none of your business).
6. Wants to have and keep a beautiful home.

I had a total of about fifteen or twenty items on my list. The rest of the list had things pertaining to physical attributes or personality. I think the other item I didn't get was long hair. At the time we met, she wore her hair short. Amia has since begun to wear her hair longer, simply because of me. Yep, she's a keeper.

INDEX

50%'ers, 42
50 percent, 13, 40

A

Amia (Mack's wife), 39
attraction-based relationships, problems with, 32–34

B

Boaz (Ruth's second husband), 11, 15–16, 18, 21, 36–37, 45–47, 53
Boaz method
  guidelines for, 46, 48, 50, 52
  steps included in
    engage, 23, 25
    investigate, 21
    provide/protect, 36, 38
    watch, 15, 17, 19
  summary of, 55

C

courting, 5, 11, 14–15, 17, 19, 24–25, 29, 31, 33, 35–37, 39–41, 45, 47, 49, 51
courtship, 31, 51
  definition of, 40
  right way of, 40–42

D

dating, 33
  Christian approach to, 29
  common idea about, 29
  difference between courtship and, 31, 40, 42
Divorce, 11, 13, 33–34, 40, 44, 54, 56

F

Foundation, 24, 42, 48

G

Genesis 2:8, 48
Genesis 2:15, 48
Genesis 2:21-24, 48
Genesis 3:6-9, 50
Gossip, 21

J

John 3:16, 36

L

Lemuel (biblical character), 22
Lisa, 19
List, the, 19, 55–56
Luke 6:45, 23
Luke 14:28-30, 24
Lust, 34, 48

M

Mack, John Alan
  courtship with Amia, 22, 24–25, 31, 35, 38–39, 44, 46, 56
  previous marriage, 10
marriage in America, 13

N

Naomi (Ruth's mother-in-law), 17, 21, 46, 53

O

Orpah (Ruth's sister-in-law), 53

P

percent, 40
Proverbs 6, 55
Proverbs 22:1, 21–22
Proverbs 23:7, 51
Proverbs 31, 22, 55
Proverbs 31:23, 22

R

Romans 12:2, 51
Ruth (biblical character), 11, 16–18, 21, 36–37, 53
Ruth 1:16, 16
Ruth 2:2, 17
Ruth 2:3, 53
Ruth 2:10, 18
Ruth 2:11, 21
Ruth 2:13, 18

S

2 Corinthians 6:14, 16
2 Timothy 3:1-6, 48

T

Thatcher, Margaret, 19

Y

Yoked, 16–17